Dominie Chapter Books

A Pocketful of Acorns

By Margaret Beames
Illustrated by Carol Daniel

Dominie Press, Inc.

Publisher: Raymond Yuen
Editor: Bob Rowland
Designer: Mark Deutman
Illustrator: Carol Daniel
Cover Designer: Carol Anne Craft

Published by:

Dominie Press, Inc.
1949 Kellogg Avenue
Carlsbad, California 92008 USA

ISBN 0-7685-0320-5

Printed in Singapore by PH Productions Pte Ltd

1 2 3 4 5 6 PH 01 00 99

TABLE OF CONTENTS

Chapter One

A Special Errand for Emily

Before school one morning, Emily's mother asked her to take some fresh-baked cookies to old Mrs. Paloma.

"Why?" asked Emily. And then, after a moment, she added, "Can I have one?" They were still warm from the oven.

Her Mom passed her the plate. "Because she's our neighbor and she's old," Mom said. "Besides, she's upset about her tree."

"What tree?" Emily asked. "Why would anyone get upset about a tree?"

"It's that big tree at the edge of her garden," her mother said. "They're going to cut it down when the new road goes through. She says she'll guard it with her life, but that won't do any good. They'll just move her out of the way."

Emily was curious about this tree. So she picked up the box of cookies her mother had prepared, grabbed her book bag, and gave her Mom a hug.

"I'll see you later," she called out as she walked down the sidewalk.

Mrs. Paloma lived down the street where the road curved sharply toward the town. It was a difficult corner for people driving their cars, but soon it would be gone. The new road that would replace it would eliminate the sharp curve.

Instead of passing in front of Mrs. Paloma's cottage, the new road would pass directly behind it. Unfortunately, it would cut off the end of Mrs. Paloma's garden where her prized tree stood.

Chapter Two

Mrs. Paloma's Adventure

Emily knocked on the cottage door. When there was no response, she walked around to the back. Mrs. Paloma was sitting on a stool at the end of her garden, resting her back against the trunk of a huge tree.

“Hi, Mrs. Paloma,” Emily called out. “Mom sent you some fresh cookies.”

“Is that you, Emily?” Mrs. Paloma asked. She could not see very well these days. “Bring them over here.” She tasted one of the treats. “Mmm, delicious. I’ll just keep them here while I guard my tree.”

“What sort of tree is it?” Emily asked. She could fit her smallest finger into the deepest grooves in the tree’s rough bark.

“An oak tree, of course,” Mrs. Paloma said, shaking her head. “What on earth do they teach you at that school of yours?!”

“Lots,” said Emily, “but we haven’t done trees yet. What’s so special about this tree, anyway?”

“It’s seventy-six years old,” said Mrs. Paloma. “I know, because I planted it myself.”

“Were you born in this house?” asked Emily.

“Dear me, no,” said Mrs. Paloma. “I can see I’ll have to explain from the beginning. Sit down while I tell you all about it.”

Emily sat on the grass and rested her arm on her book bag. Mrs. Paloma ate another cookie before beginning her story. Emily hoped it wouldn't take too long. She didn't want to be late for school.

"I'm ninety-four years old now," Mrs. Paloma said after a long silence. "I was born in another country thousands of miles away. We were very poor, but we were happy," she said.

"When I was thirteen I went to work in a big house. It was hard work, and I soon became sick of scrubbing floors and polishing furniture every day. But then I met a young man."

Mrs. Paloma's memories brought a smile to her face.

“We wanted to get married, but we had no money,” she said. “Then Jack, my young man, got the idea of emigrating–starting a new life in another country. It was our only chance to make something of our lives.”

She paused for a moment, and then continued.

"We saved enough money for our passage, packed our few possessions, and said good-bye to our families and friends. The night before we left I was so excited, I could hardly sleep. But in the morning, I was suddenly frightened."

Emily nodded. She could understand that.

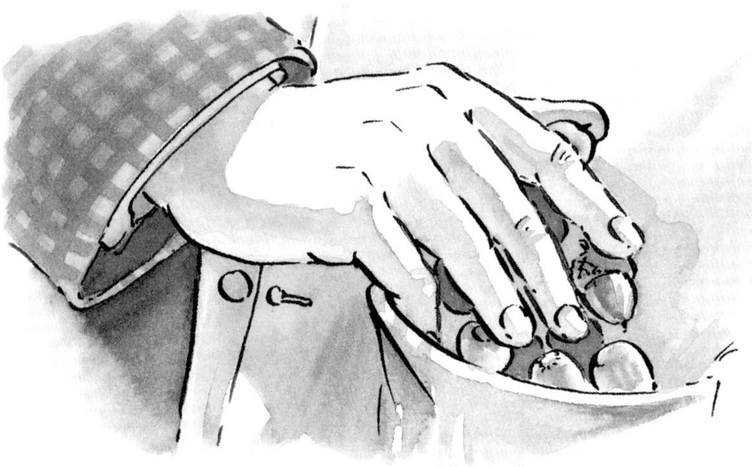

"I ran outside," Mrs. Paloma said. "I was crying. I was leaving behind so many things that I loved. Jack came to see what was wrong. He understood. We were standing under a big oak tree–hundreds of years old, it was–where he had asked me to marry him. He picked up some acorns and put them in my pocket. 'We'll plant them in our new home,' he said."

"And you did!" Emily cried.

Mrs. Paloma nodded. "I kept them safe in my pocket all the way across the ocean. And what a trip it was! I was so seasick! We went through a terrible storm on the way. And we saw whales and icebergs," she said.

"Then when we arrived in this country, we had to find jobs and a place to live."

"Is that when you came here?" asked Emily.

"That's right," said Mrs. Paloma. "Jack was a carpenter. This town was just beginning to grow."

“He found work building houses for other people. As soon as he could, he built this house for us. Our children were born here. They grew up here. And I planted those acorns here in this garden.”

She paused and dabbed her eyes.

"Well, Jack's gone now," she said, "and the children have moved away."

"But there is only one oak tree," said Emily.

"Only two of the acorns sprouted and grew into big trees," Mrs. Paloma said. "One was blown down during a terrible storm one winter. Now there's just this one left."

Mrs. Paloma suddenly looked fierce. "And if they think they're going to cut it down ..."

"Well, I think it's a shame!" cried Emily. She looked at her watch. "Golly! I'm going to be late!" she said. "I'll come and see you again."

She ran all the way to school and got there just in time.

Chapter Three

A Story That Could Save a Tree

Emily just couldn't get Mrs. Paloma's story out of her mind. The teacher scolded her twice for daydreaming. Then it was time for the students' writing exercise. The subject that day was injustice.

"Write about something you feel isn't fair," explained Mrs. Flores. "You might also explain what you think should be done about it."

Some of the children chewed their pens and groaned and sighed. But Emily knew exactly what to write about–Mrs. Paloma's tree.

She wrote as fast as she could and was amazed when Mrs. Flores said it was time to stop. She dashed off the last few words: “I don’t think it’s fair. I think we should stop them from building the road.”

After lunch, Mrs. Flores handed the students their writing exercises–all but Emily's. She called Emily up to the front of the room.

"Oh, no," thought Emily. "I'm in trouble for sloppy writing again!"

But Mrs. Flores said, "I'd like you to read your story to the class, Emily."

And so Emily read her story about Mrs. Paloma and her tree. Many of the children in the class had parents or grandparents who had emigrated. Some of the students were new to this country themselves. They knew how hard it was to settle in a strange place. Many of them kept small treasures from their native countries.

When Emily was finished, everyone had something to say.

"They can't cut down her tree!"

"No, that's a rotten thing to do!"

"Someone ought to stop them!"

"But we need the new road," Mrs. Flores pointed out.

"Why can't it go around the tree?" one child asked.

"We'll climb it and refuse to come down," said another.

"When they come with chain saws and bulldozers, we'll fight them off," said yet another.

"Calm down," said Mrs. Flores. "Maybe the town council doesn't even know about this tree."

“We could go to the council and tell them about it,” one student said.

“They wouldn’t listen,” said another. “We’re only kids.”

“Emily could read her story to the mayor,” said Ramon, one of the boys in the class.

“Yeah!” they all shouted.

“Would you, Emily?” asked Mrs. Flores.

Emily felt nervous, but she agreed to do it, if it would help save Mrs. Paloma’s tree.

Mrs. Flores called the mayor’s office. She talked for a long time and came back smiling.

"The mayor will see us at nine o'clock tomorrow morning," she said. "So be sure you're here bright and early."

Emily was so excited that night, she could hardly sleep.

"Don't get your hopes up too high," her mother warned.

Emily knew she was right. After all, grownups don't listen to children very often.

Chapter Four

A Visit with the Mayor

In the morning, Mrs. Flores led the children, two-by-two, up the street to the mall. A police officer raised his hand to stop traffic while they crossed the road.

"Good luck!" he shouted when he heard where they were going.

Other people had heard, too. Shoppers and people doing business stopped to wish them luck. A crowd had gathered outside City Hall, where the mayor had his office. Some of the children's parents were there. And there was a reporter from the local newspaper there with a camera.

The mayor was waiting for them in his office, smiling.

"It's no use," thought Emily. "To him, we're just kids doing a school project. He'll pretend to listen, but he won't do anything."

Ramon read a short speech asking the mayor to stop the road from going through Mrs. Paloma's garden.

When Ramon was finished, the mayor said, "Well now, you did the right thing in coming to see me. That's what I'm here for. But you see, it's not so easy ..."

"Emily's got something to read to you," said Ramon.

The mayor frowned. He did not like being interrupted. "Carry on then, Emily," he said with a scowl.

Emily was very nervous. But as she began to read her story, she forgot about the mayor of the town sitting there behind his desk. She forgot about the big room with its high ceilings and the stern faces in the portraits on the wall.

She remembered old Mrs. Paloma's face and how soft her eyes had been as she looked up at her tree. Emily tried her best to make them see that the tree was a link–the last link–connecting the old woman with the country in which she had grown up, and with her husband, Jack.

"I think it took a lot of courage to come all that way to a new country where they didn't know anyone," Emily said. "They worked hard and helped build this town. Mr. Paloma built a lot of the houses we live in today, and we shouldn't forget him. That's why I think we shouldn't cut down the tree," she said.

Chapter Five

A Pocketful of Acorns

Several weeks later, Emily was in Mrs. Paloma's garden again. She visited her often. The two of them weren't talking. The trucks and bulldozers building the new road were so close now that it was too noisy to be heard.

Then Mrs. Paloma led Emily into the house. She gave her a glass of cold lemonade. As they shared the cookies that Emily's mother had baked, their eyes focused on three envelopes propped up on the mantelpiece.

"I must write and thank them," said Mrs. Paloma.

She meant the mayor and the town council, who had listened after all. And the city planner who had redrawn his plans. And the farmer who had given up a strip of his land to make room for the new road. Now the road would not have to go through her garden. Her tree was safe.

"But it's thanks to you most of all," said Mrs. Paloma as Emily was leaving. Then she dropped two or three small, hard objects into Emily's pocket.

When Emily got home, she emptied her pocket. Acorns! She was puzzled for a moment. Then she smiled.

"She wants me to plant them and grow my own tree," she thought.

"And so I will!"